Coding Is </CATegorical>™

Bugs That Make Your Computer Crawl

What Are Computer Bugs?

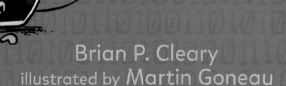

Brian P. Cleary
illustrated by Martin Goneau

M Millbrook Press • Minneapolis

All your devices require instruction—
this code's known as programming too.

It tells your computer
or web page or game
or app what it needs to do.

A **bug** is an error—a flaw in the program.
It might cause some problems like these:

ERROR X35565 INTERCE
YOUR COMPUTER WAS HALT
PLEASE RESTART THE COM

4

computers that crash and apps
that quit working
or screens that just lock up and freeze.

These **bugs** don't have wings or antennae or legs.
There aren't hives or nests where they're dwelling.

Instead, these **bugs** come from
a problem with syntax
or language or even misspelling.

Let's say you've written a code
that's instructing
this robot to wax the black car.

"Locate the car." Then "wash it" and "wax it" might be what the first commands are.

But what if you happened to type C-A-T
where you thought you had typed C-A-R?

You'd probably end up with a
cat that's upset,
instead of a freshly waxed car.

Problems with syntax—the order of words and the way they're arranged in the code—

can also cause **bugs**,
like a website that crashes
or an image or page
that won't load.

Think of the process of washing your hair.
The order of steps here is key.

How to shampoo your hair...
1. Wet hair.
2. Shampoo hair.
3. Rinse hair.
4. Dry hair.

If you rinse your hair first, then dry,
then shampoo it,
you'll fail most spectacularly!

A **bug** helps you learn what will work and what doesn't; it's one of the steps toward success.

The programmer uses a **debugging** tool that goes over code, line by line.

It then lets you know when it's
tracked down a **bug**
so it can be fixed and run fine.

If you find a **bug** in some code that you wrote, there's no need for panic or terror.

It's just like with writing or music or math:
you're simply correcting an error!

So what are bugs?

Do you know?

As you read in this book, bugs are errors in computer programs. They can cause apps to crash and screens to freeze. Coders have to learn how to debug, or locate and fix these mistakes in their code.

Here are some common computer bugs:

- misspellings
- instructions in the wrong order
- bad math
- duplicated instructions
- wrong numbers
- never-ending loops

Computer bugs are common, and you can use tools to help debug your programs. Keep in mind that block-based coding languages such as Scratch and Alice are less likely to have bugs. That's because you can drag and drop "blocks" of code to write your program, which can be helpful for beginners. Once you're comfortable with simple programs, you can write longer, more complex programs.

The best thing about coding is that anyone can do it! All you need is a computer or tablet, an internet connection, and a willingness to try.

Want to learn more?

Check out these great resources!

Books

Loya, Allyssa. *Bugs and Errors with* Wreck-It Ralph. Minneapolis: Lerner Publications, 2019.

People write code to tell computers what to do, but sometimes the code has a bug, or error. Join characters from *Wreck–It Ralph* for hands-on coding activities that will teach you about bugs in code.

Lyons, Heather. *Coding, Bugs, and Fixes*. Minneapolis: Lerner Publications, 2017.

This introduction to coding basics will walk you through algorithms, loops, bugs, and fixes. Try out your new skills with the accompanying online and off-line activities.

Prottsman, Kiki. *My First Coding Book*. New York: DK, 2017.

Practice what you've learned by lifting flaps and pulling tabs to create a code that will let you escape from a jungle, build a robot, and more!

Websites and Apps

Code.org

https://code.org

This site has lots of resources for anyone who wants to start coding—including students and their teachers. Check out the "Projects" tab to see what other kids have done, and take a look at the code for these projects.

Daisy the Dinosaur

A free iPad app, Daisy the Dinosaur teaches the basics of coding as kids drag and drop blocks of code to make Daisy the dinosaur dance.

Find activities, games, and more at
www.brianpcleary.com

ABOUT THE AUTHOR & THE ILLUSTRATOR

BRIAN P. CLEARY is the author of the best-selling Words Are CATegorical® series, as well as the Sounds Like Reading® series, the Poetry Adventures series, and several others. He is also the author of *Crunch and Crack, Oink and Whack! An Onomatopoeia Story* and *The Sun Played Hide-and-Seek: A Personification Story*. He lives in Cleveland, Ohio.

MARTIN GONEAU is the illustrator of many books, including quite a number in the Words Are CATegorical™ series. When he is not drawing, he enjoys playing video games and learning how to code. He lives in Trois-Rivières, Québec, with his lovely wife and his two sons.

Thank you to technical expert Michael Miller for reviewing the text and illustrations.

Millbrook Press
A division of Lerner Publishing Group, Inc.
241 First Avenue North
Minneapolis, MN 55401 USA

For reading levels and more information, look up this title at www.lernerbooks.com.

Main body text set in Chauncy Decaf Medium 27/36. Typeface provided by the Chank Company.
The illustrations in this book were created in Adobe Photoshop using a Wacom Cintiq Pro 16.

Library of Congress Cataloging-in-Publication Data

Names: Cleary, Brian P., 1959- author. | Goneau, Martin, illustrator.
Title: Bugs that make your computer crawl : what are computer bugs? / Brian P. Cleary ; illustrated by Martin Goneau.
Description: Minneapolis, MN : Millbrook Press, a division of Lerner Publishing Group, Inc., [2019] | Series: Coding is CATegorical | Audience: Ages 5-9. | Audience: Grades K to 3.
Identifiers: LCCN 2018026947 (print) | LCCN 2018028107 (ebook) | ISBN 9781541543843 (eb pdf) | ISBN 9781541533097 (lb : alk. paper) | ISBN 9781541545601 (pb : alk. paper)
Subjects: LCSH: Software failures—Juvenile literature. | Debugging in computer science—Juvenile literature. | Computer programs—Correctness—Juvenile literature.
Classification: LCC QA76.76.F34 (ebook) | LCC QA76.76.F34 C54 2019 (print) | DDC 005.1/4—dc23

LC record available at https://lccn.loc.gov/2018026947

Manufactured in the United States of America
1-44878-35728-10/22/2018